ACKNOWLEDGEMENTS

We wish to thank the following people for providing us with information, and for reviewing and commenting on the manuscrip during its development.

Robert S. Thompson, MD, Director, Preventive Care Research; Grou Health Cooperative of Puget Sound.

Linda Quan, MD, Chief, Emergency room, and Kenneth Feldman, MD, and the emergency room staff, Children's Orthopedic Hospitc and Medical Center of Seattle.

Paul H. Wise, MD, Director, Emergency and Primary Care Services, and John W. Craef, MD, Boston Children's Hospital Medical Cente

We would like to thank the following groups for information provided:
>   American Heart Association,
>   National Safety Council,
>   Seattle Poison Control Center, and
>   Harborview Burn Center.

We would particularly like to thank Kirk Stickels, Chief of the Monro Fire Department; Hans Dankers, MD, Family Practitioner; and Lt. Eric Andrews, Snohomish Co. Fire District Number 7 for their continued support and help throughout this project.

Parenting Press   7750 31st Ave. NE   Seattle, WA 98115

P9-DWW-126

What Would You Do If...

Written by Lory Freeman
Illustrated by Marina Megale

Introduction by Paul H. Wise, M.D.

INTRODUCTION

It often comes as a surprise to those concerned with the well-being of children to learn that injuries cause more death, pain, and serious result in children than all other conditions combined. Indeed, for a one month old child until he or she reaches middle age, the leading injuries are almost always unexpected and at times catastrophic. This has led to a recognition of two major strategies directed at reducing the impact of childhood injuries.

First, it has become increasingly clear that good initial prehospital care can dramatically improve an injured child's chance for recovery. This has meant improved emergency medical systems designed to quickly stabilize and transport children in need of emergency care. It has also meant a larger effort to educate the public in basic medical emergency procedures. The hope has been that community residents can assist each other with emergencies in coordination with organized medical services.

Who is likely to be present when a child is injured? Teachers, parents and other adults are often confronted with children in distress. Yet children themselves are most often present when an injury occurs. **What Would You Do If** is a creative effort to address this issue. Not only can children learn more about their bodies and its vulnerabilities, but they can also learn ways to provide appropriate first aid in the event of injury.

The second strategy has been one of prevention. The first step in preventing injuries is to recognize that what we usually term "accidents" are in fact, not accidental. To call these injurious events "accidents" implies they are caused by a primary element of chance. Rather, they are fairly predictable, and are related to the developmental stage of the child.

Toddlers are injured in falls, burns, drownings and poisonings. School age children are injured in sports, on bicycles and as pedestrians. Adolescents are at highest risk from motor vehicle collision, homicide and suicide. **What Would You Do If,** provides children with fundamental information regarding emergency medical conditions and their initial management. This in turn allows children the opportunity to begin to think about the determinants of injury, and explore their own activites and fears. This is perhaps the most important aspect of **What Would You Do If,** for it both recognizes and unleashes the inherent creativity and strengths of children. In this way **What Would You Do If** is truly a testament to the capabilities of children to help care for themselves and each other.

Paul H. Wise, M.D.
Director, Emergency & Primary Care Services
The Children's Hospital & Medical Center of Boston

TABLE OF CONTENTS

HOW TO USE THIS BOOK

A child leans over a campfire and her clothes catch on fire. Does she recall the STOP, DROP AND ROLL technique she has recited once a year for the last three years? No! Why not? Panic conquers the intellect! Forgetting what she has been told, she runs, fans the flames, and suffers third degree burns over 40% of her body. Why? For a child to recall proper first aid techniques in an emergency situation, technique recall must be an automatic response. Play-acting is a teaching-learning technique that helps children internalize information. That information is then readily available for instant recall at the appropriate moment. **What Would You Do If...** is written in a format which sets the stage for this "play-acting" learning environment.

Ask children "what would you do if?" for each situation. See if they have a response and if not, let them experience for a minute, feeling the anxiety of not knowing what to do. Then turn the page and read the "this is how to help" section, practicing each technique. Learning takes place more effectively when as many of the child's senses can be used in the learning process as possible. Act out the first aid techniques. Run water on a "burn," put direct pressure on each other's "cuts."

Be dramatic, fall on the floor, cry "ouch" when you "cut" yourself and ask the child for help. Have children "play-act" the situations and their appropriate first aid responses with adults, with other children, and with their dolls and stuffed animals. Repeat them often for reinforcement.

The format of **What Would You Do If...** is designed to encourage discussion of how each situation could have been prevented. Look at the pictures of the "emergency" scenes. Ask the child what they would have done so that it might not have ever happened. How could things have been different to avoid the problem? Whenever possible, encourage the child to supply the answers.

Remember, if you keep this book new and unused, a child won't know **"What Would You do If..."**

CHILDREN'S INTRODUCTION

What would you do if...

You are playing with a friend, and your friend gets hurt. Can you help?

YES!

You can help.

This book will show you what to do. Turn to page 12 to find how to help with bleeding.

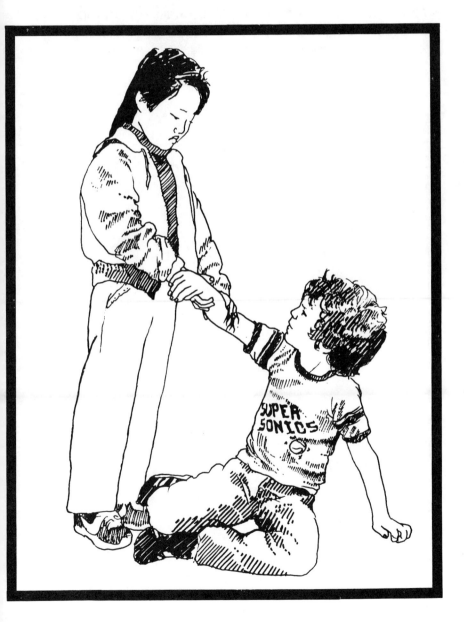

BLEEDING

What would you do if ...

You and your barefoot friend are walking on the beach. Your friend steps on a piece of glass. Your friend's foot is bleeding a lot.

This is how to help:

1. Push on the cut.

Put your hand right on the cut and push just hard enough to make the bleeding stop. Keep holding your hand on the cut. If you have something clean like a towel, scarf, or tissue, put it on the cut before you push on the cut.

2. Raise the cut.

Help your friend sit or lie down. To raise, put something under her foot so it is raised up. You can roll your coat up or put your backpack under her foot.

3. Get help.

If the bleeding is stopped and your friend can push on the cut, call or go get help.

REMEMBER:
If a cut is bleeding a lot, push directly on the cut and raise the arm or leg.

HOT LIQUID BURNS

What would you do if ...

Your mom and dad are at the neighbors stacking firewood. Your mom asks you to tell her when the pot of water on the stove starts to boil. You are playing around in the kitchen and forget to be careful. While you are playing around you bump the handle of the pan. Boiling hot water splashes out of the pot and burns your arm.

This is how to help:

1. Hold burn under water.

Immediately put your arm in cold water. You can hold it under running water or sink it in a pan of clean cold water. Keep the burn in cool water until pain stops.

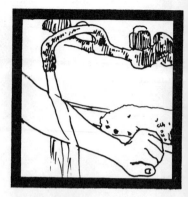

2. Call your parents.

If your burns starts to hurt when you take it out of the cool water, call your parents.

REMEMBER:
Cool a burn with cold water.

BROKEN BONES

What would you do if ...

You and a friend are riding bikes and enjoying the
wind blowing on your faces. Your friend doesn't see a
hole in the road and falls off his bike. His arm is bent
in a strange way. It hurts a lot.

This is how to help:

1. Shout for help!

2. Keep your friend exactly where he is unless he is in a dangerous place. Do not move the hurt arm (or leg). It might be broken.

3. If your friend's arm is bleeding, remember how to stop bleeding. Push your hand on the cut just hard enough to stop bleeding.

4. Go for help.

If no one has come, go for help.

REMEMBER:
Get help and do not move a broken bone.

UNCONSCIOUSNESS

What would you do if ...

You are at home with your mother and she is high up
on a ladder painting the living room. Suddenly she
slips and falls. She is lying on the ground, not moving
at all. It seems like she is asleep, but she does not
wake up when you talk to her. She is unconscious.

This is how to help:

1. Leave her alone.

Do not move her at all.

2. Shout for help.

If another grownup is home, have them help you.

3. Call the emergency number.

If no one comes immediately, go to a phone and dial the emergency number _____ .
Say, "My mom is hurt. My address is _____ .
My phone number is _____ .

REMEMBER:
Call for help, and do not move the unconscious person.

24

SOMETHING IN THE EYE

What would you do if ...

You are raking up leaves and a gust of wind blows some dust into your eye.

This is how to help:

1. DO NOT RUB your eye.

If you rub your eye, you could scratch the surface of the eye.

2. Gently grasp your upper lid and pull it gently over your lower eye lid. Now blink.

3. If this does not help, rinse your eye with water, or go ask someone for help. See page 32 to find out how to rinse your eye.

REMEMBER:
If you get something in your eye, do not rub your eye.

CHEMICAL BURNS OF THE EYE

What would you do if ...

While your father is at the neighbors, you are reaching
to get a banana off the refrigerator. You accidentally
knock some cleanser off the top of the refrigerator.
Some of it splashes into your brother's eye.

This is how to help:

1. Rinse the eye.

Quickly have him lean under the faucet while you run cold water on his hurt eye. Be sure to have him lean so that the water does not go in the other eye.

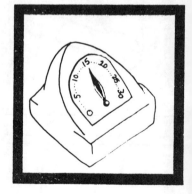

2. Call for help.

While the eye is being rinsed, call or phone a grownup.

3. Rinse for 15 minutes.

Set a kitchen timer for at least fifteen minutes if you have one.

REMEMBER:
Rinse the eye immediately.

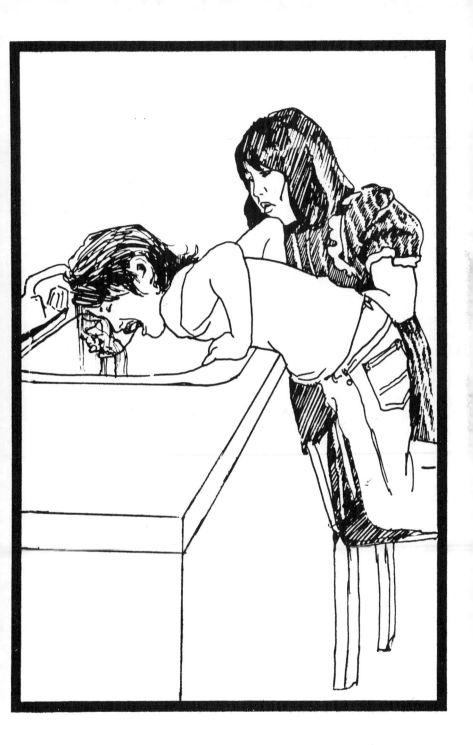

CHOKING

What would you do if ...

You are eating lunch at the park with two of your friends. Everyone is being very silly and laughing a lot. One of your friends begins to grasp his neck. He cannot breathe or talk. He is choking.

This is how to help:

1.   Lean friend forward.

2.   Slap his back.

Make a fist and hit your friend hard between the shoulder blades.

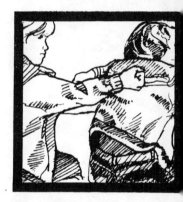

3.   Get help quickly.

Tell your other friend to go for help. She can bring a grownup back or phone the emergency number. Remind them the emergency number is

_____.

REMEMBER:

Lean friend forward and hit him between the shoulder blades.

NOSE BLEED

What would you do if ...

You are playing ball with your brother. The ball hits you in the nose. Your nose starts to bleed.

This is how to help:

1. Pinch your nose.

2. Lean forward.

While you are pinching your nose together, lean forward.

3. Hold for five minutes.

Continue to pinch your nose for at least five minutes before you check to see if the bleeding has stopped.

4. Check for bleeding.

If the nose is bleeding when you check, pinch nose for a longer time. Check again. If it is still bleeding, go ask for help.

REMEMBER:
Pinch your nose and lean forward.

ELECTRICAL SHOCK

What would you do if ...

You and your little sister are cutting and gluing paper in your bedroom. All of a sudden your little sister turns and sticks the scissors in the electric outlet. She screams and seems to be "stuck" to the scissors and the outlet.

This is how to help:

1. LEAVE HER ALONE!

Do not touch her. If you touch her you will get shocked too. Then you will not be able to help her.

2. Call for help immediately.

Ask the grownup to knock her away with a wooden pole or turn off the electricity in the house.

REMEMBER:
DO NOT TOUCH anyone who is getting an electric shock. Call for help.

INSECT STING

What would you do if ...

You are outside picking some flowers for your mother and a bee stings you on your arm. It hurts!

This is how to help:

1. Call for help.

If you know that you are allergic to bee stings, go for help or call for help immediately.

2. Run cold water on bite.

Run cold water on the bee sting or hold a cool, wet washcloth on the sting.

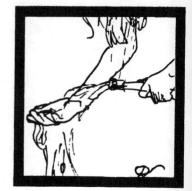

REMEMBER:
Run cool water on an insect bite.

SNAKE BITE

What would you do if ...

You and your friend are climbing rocks. All of a sudden your friend cries out in pain. A snake has bitten her!

This is how to help:

1. Keep bite low.

Have your hurt friend lie down very still. If the bite is on the arm, hand, leg or foot, keep it lower than her heart. (Heart is in the chest.)

2. Be calm.

Tell your friend not to worry. You can say, "Don't worry. Lie still until I get back. I will go get a grownup to help."

3. Get help.

Shout for help, or go get someone as quickly as you can.

(Many snakes are not poisonous. But if you are not sure about the one that bites you or a friend, follow these instructions.)

REMEMBER:
Keep snake bite low and get help.

POISONING

What would you do if ...

Your parents are next door helping a neighbor move his refrigerator. You are taking care of your little brother. You aren't watching him as closely as you should. Suddenly he walks out of the bathroom with a bottle in his hand and says, "Funny candy." You notice the bottle is a pill bottle.

This is how to help:

1. Remove the poison.

Keep the bottle so you can tell the poison control center what he ate.

2. Give him water.

Quickly get a drink of water. Tell him to drink it. If he cannot do it by himself **do not** make him.

3. Call your parents.

If you cannot reach your parents call the emergency number and the poison control center. (See your Emergency Phone Card.)

REMEMBER:
When someone swallows something poisonous, dial the emergency number **and** the poison control center number.

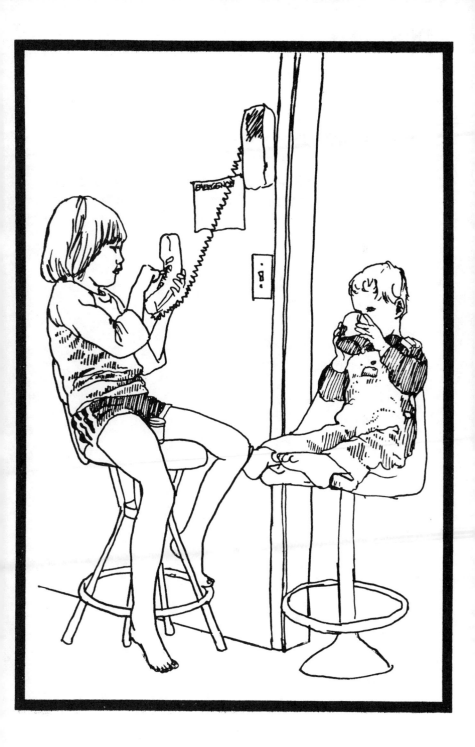

DOG BITE

What would you do if ...

While you are walking home from school, you drop
your papers. As you pick them up, a dog runs out of
a nearby yard and bites you.

This is how to help:

1. Remember what the dog looks like.

Look at the dog and remember what it looks like. How big is it? What color is it? Does it have long hair or short hair?

2. Push on bite.

If the bite is bleeding a lot, press on the bite just hard enough to stop the bleeding.

3. Call for help.

Shout for help. If you live nearby and there is a parent at home, tell them what happened and what the dog looks like.

REMEMBER:
If a dog bites you, remember what it looks like and tell a grownup as soon as you can.

CLOTHES ON FIRE

What would you do if ...

You and your family are roasting marshmallows around a campfire. Your marshmallow catches on fire. When you wave the marshmallow around to put out the fire, it drops off the stick and onto your pants. Your pant leg catches on fire.

This is how to help:

1.   STOP.

Stay right where you are. Do
not run!

2.   DROP!

Fall to the ground immediately.

3.   ROLL!

Roll on the ground to put out
the fire.

4.   Call for water.

If someone is near, tell them to
get water and pour it on the
clothes.

REMEMBER:

Stop, drop and roll if your
clothes are on fire.

HOW TO PHONE FOR HELP

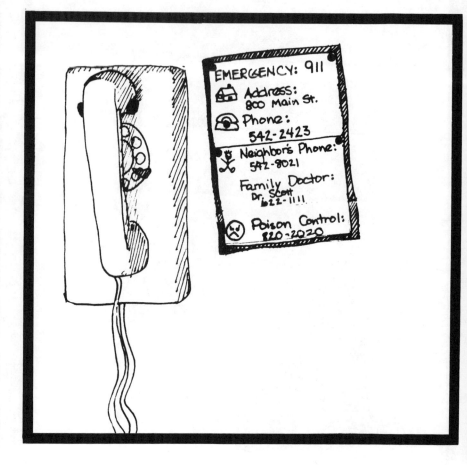

Have an adult help you practice dialing your emergency number on a toy phone, or the real phone with the hook pressed down.

ONLY DIAL THE EMERGENCY NUMBER WHEN YOU REALLY NEED HELP.

The person who answers the emergency phone must be able to answer the call of someone who really needs help.

Have someone help you fill out the emergency card on page 71, and hang it near your phone.

This is how to use the phone:

1. Dial _____ .

Dial your emergency number.
(Write your emergency number
above.)

**2. Give address and phone
number.**

Say, "My address is

_____ . "

(Fill in your address)
"My phone number is

_____ . "

(Fill in phone number.)

3. Tell them your problem.

Say, "I need help because..."
and then tell them your
problem. **Do not** hang up until
the person answering the
phone says it is okay to hang
up.

REMEMBER:
Tell your address, phone
number, and then your problem.

YOU CAN HELP!

Practice all the ways you can help a hurt friend. Have a friend pretend to be hurt. See if you can remember what to do.

REMEMBER:
If you are with your friend and someone gets hurt, YOU CAN HELP! Have fun learning.

EMERGENCY PHONE CARD

EMERGENCY:

🏠 Address:

☎ Phone:

👤 Neighbor's Phone:

Family Doctor:

☹ Poison Control:

71

EMERGENCY:

🏠 Address:

☎ Phone:

Neighbor's Phone:

Family Doctor:

Poison Control:

EMERGENCY:

Address:

Phone:

Neighbor's Phone:

Family Doctor:

Poison Control:

PICTORIAL INDEX

ALPHABETICAL INDEX

PARENTS' REFERENCE BOOKS

A Sigh of Relief, The First-Aid Handbook for Childhood Emergencys, produced by Martin I. Green, 1979, Bantam Books.

Standard First Aid and Personal Safety, prepared by the American National Red Cross, 1979, Doubleday and Co.